Practical Solutions for Busy Lives

(keeping little hands busy)

BARBOUR
PUBLISHING

© 2004 by Barbour Publishing, Inc.

Written by Rebecca Currington, Deborah Ann Valdez, and Vicki J. Kuyper in conjunction with Snapdragon Editorial Group, Inc.

ISBN 1-59310-212-7

Illustrations © Mary Lynn Blasutta.

Published by Barbour Publishing, Inc., P.O. Box 719, Uhrichsville, Ohio 44683
www.barbourbooks.com

Our mission is to publish and distribute inspirational products offering exceptional value and biblical encouragement to the masses.

 Member of the
Evangelical Christian
Publishers Association

Printed in China.
5 4 3 2 1

Contents

Section 6: *Let Me Entertain You*

Section 7: *Thank You for My Family*

Section 8: *Happy Holidays*

Section 9: *Big Bag of Activities*

Introduction

What were you dreaming about as you carried your firstborn—sweet giggles, baby-soft kisses, wistful moments of mutual adoration? Then you became a mom and reality came crashing in. Sure, life included all the wonderful things you imagined about your baby. Trouble is, those moments are wedged tightly between diaper changes, midnight feedings, constant vigilance, and utter exhaustion. Motherhood is just plain hard work, especially in the early years.

We've designed this *Moms on the Move* book, *Keeping Little Hands Busy*, specifically to help you meet just a few of the challenges of this great institution we call Motherhood. Along with the ideas, we've given detailed instructions and lists of the materials you will need. We've also included an inspiring story to keep your mother's heart sparkling bright.

The Great Outdoors

Whether you live in the city or the country, your kids will benefit from time spent outdoors. The fresh air, exercise, and opportunity for imaginative play are a great counterbalance to time spent in front of the television, computer, or video game console. Try some of these outdoor activity ideas, and you might spark a lifelong love of nature in your kids!

Word to the Wise: Parents can use the "great outdoors" as a learning laboratory on God's creation.

Backyard Butterfly Hunt

Children love nothing more than to run around the yard with the breeze in their hair and sun on their faces. A *butterfly hunt* is the perfect opportunity to do just that. Your little ones may not actually capture a butterfly, but that's just fine—the fun is in the pursuit.

Before your hunt begins, gather a few pictures of colorful butterflies from books, magazines, and encyclopedias (the Internet is a great source). Cut each butterfly out of the picture and scatter your colorful collection around the table. Then set your children down with paper, glue, and crayons. Let them glue the butterflies to the paper, draw and color their own. Encourage them to use bright colors and create to their hearts' content. Then build your nets and head out to the yard or a nearby park to find the real thing.

Word to the Wise: Tell your children that butterflies are like their dreams—they must never stop chasing them.

- Bright crayons (the smaller the child, the bigger the crayon needs to be)
- White paper
- Glue
- Nine pipe cleaners per net (bright colors are best)
- One pair of old opaque pantyhose (makes two nets)
- Stapler

Whether you are entertaining one child or half a dozen, this can be a great adventure for a lovely spring or summer afternoon. Let your children run and tiptoe and swoosh. If a butterfly does happen into the net, encourage your child to set it free. Typically, little ones won't want to do this. Use it as an opportunity to teach them about kindness to all God's creatures.

- Lay two pipe cleaners side by side.

- Scoot the end of one up 1 inch and twist them together, leaving an inch of single pipe at each end.

- Repeat this process until you have three doubled pipes.

- Twist the single end of a pipe to the single end of the next pipe until you have one long pipe.

- Cut the pantyhose 2–3 inches above the heel.

- Lay the pipe cleaner inside the pantyhose and roll the edges around the pipes.

- Staple the pantyhose to the pipe cleaners.

- Lay three more pipe cleaners side by side evenly.

- Twist them together.

- Attach the ends to the hoop, twist, and staple.

Make It Memorable

This is one activity that begs to be recorded. If you have a camcorder be sure to take it along. If not, take a camera. (Disposable cameras work just as well as the expensive kind.) Post the butterfly pictures the children created on bedroom walls or with magnets on the refrigerator.

another
great Idea

Caterpillar Caper

Most children find bugs charming. Finding them disgusting or frightening is generally a response they learn from adults.

Tell your children that when a butterfly egg hatches, a tiny caterpillar crawls out. Some caterpillars are green and gray so that they can hide in the leaves of a bush or tree. But others are bright colors—reds, oranges, yellows. They are long like worms and scoot along on three pairs of legs. Each caterpillar has six eyes on each side of its head. Caterpillars are soft and fluffy, so it isn't wise to handle them.

Just like with the butterfly adventure, prepare your children by helping them make their own paper caterpillars at the kitchen table. Then they will be ready to take the caper outdoors in search of the real thing.

Word to the Wise: Children are like caterpillars—though immature, they hold the promise of future glory.

- Construction paper
- Scissors
- Glue
- Crayons or markers
- Pipe cleaners
- Small flashlight
- White cloth; 2 feet by 2 feet is ideal

This outdoor activity works best in the spring and early summer. Lay the white cloth under a small tree or bush or garden plants. Ask the children to shake the plant, bush, or tree vigorously. Then check the cloth for caterpillars. When you find one, leave it on the cloth (tiny hands are prone to squeeze too tightly). Let the children examine their find right there on the cloth with the flashlight. Allow them to touch the caterpillar very carefully and watch it wriggle across the cloth.

- Lay your finger on the construction paper and let your child trace around it with a crayon or marker. The child can use his or her own finger, as well.

- Cut out your creepy crawlers.

- Glue them to another piece of construction paper.

- Color them with crayons or markers.

- Cut up pipe cleaners and let the children glue them to their creepy crawlers as legs and feelers.

another
great *Idea*

MOM
Meditations

Your children are just as delicate as those tiny, fluffy caterpillars. They must be handled with care and fed large portions of love, encouragement, and approval if they are to become all that God has created them to be. Enjoy them while they are in your care, for one day not so long from now, they will burst and fly.

Sunshine Campout

Children love the idea of camping, but often small children are too intimidated by the darkness to enjoy an overnight in the backyard. So put up your tent and let your kids bask in the sun rather than under the stars. The best time of the year for this activity is fall, when the outdoor temperatures are moderate.

Plan your sunshine campout the same way you would an overnight. Cover the bottom of the tent with blankets or sleeping bags. Let your children carry in their favorite books and stuffed animals. Let each child prepare his or her own lunch. Suggested: a peanut butter and jelly sandwich, a box of raisins, and a juice box or drink in a plastic water bottle. Provide each child with a small flashlight to play with inside the tent. Count on it, leaves and dirt will get tracked into the tent, so use old blankets and pillowcases.

Once you've completed the preparations, let your children play in the tent to their heart's content. At naptime, allow them to rest on their sleeping bags. Every thirty minutes to an hour, pop in and join the fun!

Word to the Wise: God covers us with His love when we put our trust in Him.

- Tent
- Sleeping bag or blankets
- Pillows
- Sack lunch and snacks
- Juice boxes or empty water bottles
- Books, stuffed animals, soft toys
- Small flashlights

CAUTION!

- Avoid breakable toys or toys with small parts.
- Glass bottles and metal cans pose a significant hazard.
- Place the tent near an open window or door so you can hear what is going on. Remember, you won't be able to see what is happening.
- Check on the children often.
- Never allow candles or matches or any flammable substance.
- Always be aware of the temperature inside the tent.

Many activities, including the Sunshine Campout, work best with a minimum of structure. Allow your children to play freely, enjoying the option to explore, improvise, and develop their imaginations. When you join the fun, go along with what is in progress rather than starting a new thing.

another **g r e a t** *Idea*

$ Cost Savers

Tents can be costly if you are on a tight budget. For the purposes of this activity, an improvised tent will work just as well. Hang a tarp, sheet, blanket, or an old tablecloth between two lawn chairs or from the low hanging branches of a tree. Just be sure your rigging won't pose a danger for your children.

If you decide to purchase a tent, look for a used one at a garage sale or estate sale. You might also try a Goodwill or army surplus store for a good bargain.

Overcoming Obstacles

An obstacle course is great fun—and more. It can provide a healthy dose of exercise and an opportunity to improve balance, dexterity, and other physical skills. It can become a permanent part of your backyard or a temporary setup. Either way, your children will enjoy the challenge.

Take care to create a course that is suitable for the ages of your children. For young children, emphasize running, jumping, and crawling. You may be inclined to build a sophisticated setup, but a simple course works just as well.

Line the sides of your running track with Styrofoam or brightly colored tape. Let the grass grow up and mow through it to create a track. You can even use fall leaves to outline the path. Give your track as many twists and turns as possible. One or two old tires can provide an opportunity to learn some fancy footwork. Place lightweight lawn chairs side by side and let the children crawl through the legs.

Word to the Wise: Encourage your children to follow you through the course, just as they will be following you through life.

Items Needed:

- Old tire
- Lawn chairs
- Brightly colored tape
- Whistle
- Timer
- Notebook for keeping records

INSTRUCTIONS

Lead your children through the course several times before asking them to go it alone. When they have become familiar with the elements, line them up and let them have a try at it. Blow the whistle when each child begins, time his or her completion on the course, and record the result so each child can see his or her progress. Note where each child is challenged so you can give special encouragement in that area.

Some children are naturals when it comes to physical activities, and some are not. Avoid competitions that might frustrate young participants. Instead, encourage your children to improve their own records and heap on lots of enthusiasm and praise.

According to statistics, obesity has become an increasing health risk for children. Exposing your children to the joys and rewards of physical exercise and conditioning at an early age can set in place a lifelong habit that promotes health and well-being.

CAUTION!

- Never use bricks, rocks, or other hard objects to line the running track.

- Grassy tracks are best for younger children. They will get plenty of grass stains on their clothing, so dress them accordingly.

- Provide plenty of water (room temperature) for your young athletes.

- Beware of rising temperatures and too much time in the sun. (Don't forget sunscreen.)

- Always be there to supervise this activity.

Good
IDEA

If you don't have a backyard, this activity can be as easy as a trip to the park. Set up your course on a flat area and let your children run and jump and crawl. Odds are, you will attract the attention of other youngsters who will also want to participate in your fun.

another
great
Idea

Dads often have less time to spend with their kids than moms—but a little planning can make that time extra special for the kids. Whether indoors or outdoors, making things or just observing the world, the following activities will provide lifelong memories for your kids—and their dad. And they'll give you a little time to accomplish something else, whether that's cleaning the house or taking a nap!

THINGS TO DO WITH DADDY

Things to Do with Daddy

Word to the Wise: Moms, here's a tremendous opportunity to help your husbands be Ephesians 6:4 kinds of guys: "Fathers. . .bring [your children] up in the training and instruction of the Lord."

Bathtub Fishermen

Dads, kids, and fishing poles have been a time-honored tradition for generations. Trouble is, it's not so easy to find a lake these days—or even a pond. But there are options. Almost everyone has a bathtub, where Daddy and the kids can practice their technique and have a lot of fun doing it.

While you're waiting for Dad to get home from work, put the kids at the kitchen table with the following items:

Items Needed:

- Crayons or markers
- Styrofoam plates
- Glue
- Scissors
- Self-adhesive magnets (small)
- Stapler

Word to the Wise: Moms often serve as key communicators in the house, but time spent with Dad encourages little ones to share their thoughts and ideas with him, too.

Encourage the children to color the plates with bright colors. Put two plates together and cut a piece out of the middle in the shape of a fish. Attach a magnet to the white side of one of the fish halves. Put the two white sides of the fish together and glue the edges. Follow this up by stapling the edges.

After dinner, Dad can help the children with their poles. He will need:

- 1-foot dowel rod for each pole
- Yarn (try to choose a different color for each child)
- Glue
- 1 clothespin for each pole
- Scissors
- Glue
- Self-adhesive magnets (small)

INSTRUCTIONS

Glue the yarn securely to the end of the dowel rod. Then tie the end of the piece of yarn to the clothespin. Attach one of the magnets to the clothespin. Put no more than a couple of inches of water in the bathtub and throw in the fish. Now you're ready. Have a basket or plastic bowl ready to put the fish in as they are caught. This fishing activity can easily merge with bath time.

Make It Memorable

Punch a hole in the nose of each fish and thread a 2-foot piece of yarn through the holes. Use the color each child selected for his or her pole. This makes determining ownership easy. Double up the yarn and tie the ends together. Let your fishermen display the stringers with fish in their rooms. An easy way is to tie the yarn around the doorknob. This will also ensure that you can find the fish the next time Dad and the kids want to do a little fishin'.

another
great Idea

Birdwatching for Babes

Introducing your children to the world of birds could stir an interest that lasts a lifetime. Regardless of your location or the season of the year, birds are plentiful. Their beauty and variety provide an ideal project for dads and youngsters.

Some men are handy with a hammer and saw; for those dads, building a birdhouse or birdfeeder will be a simple task. But this activity can easily be managed even by those dads whose talents and skills run to other disciplines.

Word to the Wise: Remind little ones that God watches out for each of us just as He watches out for each bird.

Items Needed:

- Old magazines

- Plastic milk jugs

- Sturdy twine

- Glue

- Crayons or markers

- Scissors

- Bag of birdseed

- Bird book listing common species

- Small notebook and pencil

INSTRUCTIONS

Dad should cut the top from a milk jug with scissors or a pocket knife. Then the children can cut out pictures of birds or draw and color their own to glue to the sides of the container. The twine should be tied to the handle of the jug. Then fill the jug with seed and tie it to a tree branch. Hang another jug with water near the first. Place it near a window so you and the children can watch the action together.

another great Idea

Once the winged ones discover the bird feeder, they will come flying. Don't expect delicate table manners and birds coming and going in an orderly fashion. Birds are messy. They will flock to the feeder as long as the seed lasts and spill as much as they carry away. The children won't be bored. Once the frenzy begins, have Dad and the kids find comfortable places by the window or outside on a blanket. Use the bird book to identify the birds and write their names in the notebook, along with the date.

Make It Memorable

Purchase a disposable camera and let the children take turns photographing the birds they identify while you are on your birdwatching outing. Of course, these will not be magazine quality, but the point is not to have a remarkable photograph but rather delighted children. A simple picture album with plastic overlays can provide a running history of your birdwatching outings.

Fabulous Frames
(A Gift for Mom)

Mother's Day can be daunting for many dads—coming up with a gift idea, loading up the kids and taking them to the mall, managing the wrapping. Better idea: *You* head to the mall and leave Dad and the kids at home to prepare homemade gifts that you are sure to love.

Items Needed:

- A favorite picture of each child
- Crayons and markers
- Popsicle sticks
- Poster board or card stock
- Craft glue
- Scissors
- Puffy paint or glitter pens
- Self-adhesive magnets
- Butcher block paper or white wrapping paper
- Clear tape

Word to the Wise: Mother's Day is an ideal opportunity for dads and kids to come together and thank you. Enjoy the day and whatever gifts they offer. You've earned it!

INSTRUCTIONS

Help the children glue card stock or poster board to the back of the picture for support. Before handing over the glue, have the children write their names on the back of their pictures: To Mom, From (child's name) and below that the child's age. Turn the picture over and glue Popsicle sticks around the edges to create the frame.

Cover the picture with a piece of poster board to protect it while the children are using the paint and pens. Accidents *do* happen! When the paint is dry, attach the magnets to the backs of the pictures and remove the protective poster board.

great another Idea

Make It Memorable

To make the gifts even more special, use the poster board and glue to create a small slot in the back under the child's name and age. Have your child write or dictate a letter to Mom on a regular sheet of stationery. Ask each child to think about what he or she likes best about Mom. Fold the letter and slip it into the slot on the back of the frame. Mom will have a gift she will treasure long after the children are grown.

Tent Town Sleepover

Little ones love this chance to camp out with Dad in the comfort and security of their own bedroom or family room. And even though it may mean multiple nights sleeping on the floor for Dad, it is most beneficial when the sleepover includes just one child at a time.

Preparing for your Tent Town Sleepover is simple. Choose an area of the house that will provide the maximum alone time. Set up a small tent or create one with a comforter or blanket and fill it with sleeping bags or pillows and comforters. Let your child choose his or her favorite books or stuffed animals.

At bedtime, Daddy and child should sneak off to their tent town for the night. Dad should use this time to recall the day the child was born, any humorous stories about him or her, and the special qualities he sees in the child. Encourage them to share jokes and songs and prayers—anything the two of them can come up with to personalize the activity and create a strengthened bond between them.

Word to the Wise: This activity is all about one-on-one time. Imagine the excitement each of your children will feel when he or she thinks, "Daddy picked me to camp out with!"

- A tent or comforter
- Pillows and blankets
- Books and toys
- Hugs, kisses, and laughs

Dad may be inclined to slip out and wander off to his own bed once the little one is asleep. If so, encourage him to stay the distance. Your child will enjoy waking up with Dad just as much as going to sleep with him.

MOM *Meditations*

You might not think that a Tent Town Sleepover can have a positive influence on your child's image of God. But it can! A child who has a strong, loving, personal relationship with his or her father is likely to respond favorably to the concept of God as a heavenly Father. He understands that God can be both strong and gentle, a firm disciplinarian and a tender shepherd.

another great *Idea*

Strike Up the Band

A love for music is one of the greatest gifts you can give your children. And early exposure has more benefits than you might imagine. Just listening and playing along can help your children develop an "ear" for music, an internalizing of pitch, rhythm, and tone. You never know when you might be inspiring a future musical prodigy. Begin by helping your children create these simple instruments.

Word to the Wise: The person who learns to appreciate music as a child almost always becomes a music lover for life.

Rain Stick

Items Needed:

- Mailing tube
- Tape
- Old nails, screws, unpopped popcorn, beads, sand, gravel
- Wrapping paper
- Crayons or markers
- Stickers
- Glue

Fill the tube ⅔ of the way to the top, and then seal it with sturdy tape. Let the children decorate the tube with the crayons and markers. Move the tube from side to side and ask the children to identify what they hear. Does it sound like rain? Let each child experiment with the rain stick for a few minutes.

Good IDEA

Many other instruments are easy to make—cymbals from disposable tin foil pie plates, rhythm sticks from wooden spoons, or drums from oatmeal or coffee containers. Let your musical imagination and your children's ingenuity guide you.

Tambourine

Items Needed:

- Two Styrofoam plates
- Hole puncher
- Several pieces of colorful yarn or ribbon
- Crayons, markers, or stickers
- Scissors
- Beans
- Stapler

INSTRUCTIONS

Have your children decorate the plates with their artwork. Then place the two plates together—tops facing each other. Using the hole puncher, make ten corresponding holes around the edges of the plates. Weave the yarn or ribbon through the holes and tie it off, allowing the extra to hang down. Place the beans in the cavity formed by the plates and staple the edges together.

Guitar

Items Needed:

- Shoe box with lid
- Five rubber bands of differing widths
- Scissors
- Crayons and markers
- Heavy white paper
- Glue or glue stick

Cover the shoe box with the white paper and glue it in place. Let your children decorate the box by drawing horses, cows, and cowboys. Cut a hole in the shoe box lid. Run the glue stick around the inside of the box lid and then put it on the box, running your hand around the top to secure the lid. Place the rubber bands across the length of the box—smallest to largest. Each rubber band will provide a different pitch.

Kazoo

Items Needed:

- A paper towel roll
- Waxed paper
- Glue or glue stick
- Crayons, markers, or stickers
- Sturdy rubber band
- Sharpened pencil
- Heavy white paper

INSTRUCTIONS

Glue the white paper to the paper towel roll. Let the kids do the decorating. Place waxed paper over one end of the roll and secure it with the rubber band. With the pencil, punch two or three holes in the waxed paper.

Good IDEA

When your band instruments are complete, let the children make their choices. Find a suitable station on the radio and join in. If you have a tape recorder, you can even take the kids outside for their music play-along. Appoint yourself the conductor and teach the children to blend the sounds of their instruments together. After a few minutes, ask one of the children to play a solo.

another great Idea

It's really true. The way to a kid's heart is through his or her stomach! Your children will enjoy the preparation, as well. Put these easy, often-on-hand ingredients on the table and let your little ones fix it up just the way they like it.

Word to the Wise: A mom's primary job is providing nourishment. Make sure your children have well-fed bodies, minds, and souls.

Worms in Mud

Ants on a Log

Items Needed:

- Instant chocolate, vanilla, or banana cream pudding
- Gummy worms
- Milk

Items Needed:

- Celery sticks (about 2 inches long)
- Peanut butter
- Raisins

Kids Can Too!

The children can put the peanut butter on the celery sticks with their fingers. Give out the raisins and let the children position them as they please on the peanut butter.

INSTRUCTIONS

Mix the pudding and pour it into bowls or pudding cups. Then let the children stir in the worms.

Cinnamon Toast

Items Needed:

- Bread
- Butter or margarine
- Sugar
- Cinnamon

Cover your table with a cloth or waxed paper. Then lay out the bread and let your little ones paint the bread with butter. (This can be done with butter knives or even chubby little fingers.) Put the sugar in a small bowl and let the kids sprinkle it on the bread. Then add a light covering of cinnamon. Place on a cookie sheet and broil for about 2 minutes.

Sunshine Cups

Items Needed:

- 4 slices of fresh bread
- Butter
- 4 eggs
- Muffin pan

Hand out the bread—one piece per person—and let the children carefully remove the crust and butter one side. Press the bread butter side down into the muffin pan. Break an uncooked egg onto each piece of bread. Bake at 350° for 20–25 minutes.

Make It Memorable

Eggs are wonderful conversation starters. While it may still be early for a little mind to get around the concept that some eggs are for eating and others are for hatching chicks, children ages 2 or 3 will begin seeing images of both on television or in books. Consider how you might explain why there is no chicken in the egg. Or teach children "soft hands" by showing them how to tenderly handle an egg. This phrase can be useful later on when kids handle kittens or puppies.

Pooh Logs

Give children half a hot dog bun and have them cover the top with peanut butter. Let them position sliced bananas on top of the peanut butter. Drizzle with honey, raisins, and sunflower seeds.

Items Needed:

- Hot dog buns
- Peanut butter
- Bananas
- Honey
- Raisins or sunflower seeds

Good
IDEA

Use pita bread, tortillas, or graham crackers as an alternative to the buns.

Appley Sauce

Items Needed:

- 4 medium apples
- 1 tbsp. brown sugar
- 1 tsp. cinnamon or apple pie spice

INSTRUCTIONS

Wash and core apples. Cut into nickel-sized pieces. Cook until soft. Add brown sugar and cinnamon or apple pie spice.

another great Idea

MOM Meditations

A mother is the primary provider of food for her children—food for their bodies, food for their minds, and food for their souls. Your children will take in all that you give them—your moods, your attitudes, your words. Be sure you feed them those things that lead to life and health.

Rainy days have gotten a bad rap over the years. Who says bad weather must make for a boring day? A little creativity will go a long way toward making rainy days fun. . .and your kids may long remember the effort you put into their activities. Don't look at rainy days as the enemy—look at them as an opportunity!

RAINY
DAYS

Word to the Wise: The extra effort you put into imaginative ideas for your kids may pay great dividends in their own creative development.

Indoor Flower Garden

Good old-fashioned dirt has great appeal for children. They love to touch it, work it with their hands, and find ways to play with it. Planting an *indoor flower garden* can be the perfect solution for rainy days when playing outside is not an option.

Before you present this idea to your little ones, choose a spot that will be easy to clean up without putting unrealistic restrictions on the children's fun. This might be a tiled floor in the entryway or kitchen, a corner of the garage, even the bathtub.

Word to the Wise: Tell your children that they are like the seeds they are planting. With time, they will grow to be the wonderful people God created them to be.

- Several packages of flower seeds
  (Choose varieties that do well indoors
  and have a picture of the flower on
  the front.)

- Medium-sized clay pot with drainage
  saucer for each child

- Crayons, markers, or stickers

- Small- to medium-sized bag of
  potting soil

- Medium plastic or aluminum bowl

- Small water pitcher or teapot

- Newspapers

It's healthy for children to participate in activities that require delayed gratification. It teaches them patience. Remind them to water their plants every day and check for signs of growth. When the flowers do appear, let your child snap a picture of his or her triumph, even if it is just a wee blossom.

INSTRUCTIONS

- Spread the newspapers over the predetermined work area.

- Pass out the pots and markers and let the children decorate the pots with their names and artwork.

- Pour part of the potting soil into the bowl.

- Let the children fill the bottom half of their pots with soil and pack it down.

- Before opening the package of seeds, let the children spend as much time as they would like studying the picture on the front of the package.

- Give each child 4–5 seeds from the packet of their choice. (It's just fine to mix seeds from several packets.)

- Instruct the children to carefully place the seeds in their pots.

- Fill the remainder of the pot with soil.

- Let the children water their plants.

- Set the pots on the windowsill.

another great Idea

Moms on the Move

Dress-Up Affair

It's no secret that girls like to play dress up, but you may be surprised to discover that boys do, too. Your girls might opt for a delicate "grown-up-lady" outfit, suitable for a fine tea party, while your boys may pursue the perfect pirate attire. Regardless, dressing up can be great fun for everyone.

Children, especially younger children, generally care more for the accessories than the actual dress or costume. An application of Mom's makeup, a simple updo for the hair, and a variety of costume jewelry will keep girls happy. If they do want to go a little more "all out," an old party dress is a good choice. It might be wise to shorten the skirt to avoid a tripping hazard. Wraparound ties and safety pins are fine for modifying the bodice.

Boys seem to care most about having something to wave in the air. A rubber sword and an eye patch will typically keep a little guy occupied for hours.

In most cases, face paint is preferable to a mask or any other headgear that would obstruct your child's vision.

Good IDEA

Scout out garage sales and thrift shops for dress-up outfits and accessories. Keep your eyes open for gaudy belts, beads, and jewelry. Snatch up interesting hats and shoes, as well. Old prom dresses or bridesmaid dresses are great buys.

Kids Can Too!

Kids are great at putting together their own costumes. Take them with you when you go to garage sales and thrift stores to look for dress-up items. It will be great fun to be together. With a little help, even the younger children can spot real treasures.

Moms on the Move

another great Idea

Creepy Crawlies

Picture this: a cold, rainy day, nothing to do, the kids whiny and bored. Doesn't that sound like the perfect time to clear off the kitchen table and invite your kids to fashion their very own creepy crawly things? Let each of your children choose one or more slimy creatures.

Try posting or attaching the critters to a blank kitchen, playroom, or bedroom wall and see it come to life. Talk about what you like and dislike about real insects or use the opportunity to share bite-sized pieces of information on the vast insect world. It's never too early to learn that spiders have eight legs but ants only have six.

Word to the Wise: Children who fear bugs can find new appreciation for studying the insect world after constructing their own creatures.

Awesome Ants

Items Needed:

- Construction paper
- Black finger paint
- Markers or crayons
- Pipe cleaners
- Scissors
- Glue

INSTRUCTIONS

Dip one finger in black paint. Then make three finger prints on the construction paper. The black spots are the ants' bodies. Draw on legs and other attachments, or cut the pipe cleaners and glue on.

Slippery Snakes

Items Needed:

- Paper plate
- Scissors
- Crayons or markers

INSTRUCTIONS

Starting on the edge of the paper plate, draw a spiral, ending in the center. Have the children color the plates their favorite snake colors. Then let them cut along the spiral line. When they reach the center, they will have a snake.

Ugly Octopus

Items Needed:

- Stocking cap
- 8 old socks or neckties
- Yarn
- Buttons
- Glue

INSTRUCTIONS

Stuff the top of the socks or ties into the stocking cap. Tie the yarn around the lower part of the cap to hold the "tentacles" together. Glue on the buttons to create eyes.

Lady Bug Land

Items Needed:

- Black and red cardstock
- Scissors
- Glue

INSTRUCTIONS

Cut several 2-inch circles from the black cardstock. Then cut 1-inch circles from the red cardstock. Cut the red circles in half. Glue them to either side of the black circles to create wings. Add another small red circle for the head and small black circles for spots on the wings.

Love Bugs

Items Needed:

- Yellow construction paper
- Pipe cleaners
- Scissors
- Popsicle sticks
- Glue
- Crayons or markers

INSTRUCTIONS

Fold the construction paper and, beginning on the fold, cut a piece in the shape of a heart with a wide base. Open up the wings and glue them to the back of the stick. Cut out a heart-shaped piece of paper (not on the fold) for the face. Glue it onto the stick. Cut and bend the pipe cleaners to the right size and glue to the back side of the stick behind the head.

50

Make It Memorable

Create a collage by gluing all the Creepy Crawlies onto a piece of poster board. Date it and let the children add their names. Then hang it in a spot where you can all enjoy it.

another great Idea

Teach Me Something New

f you're like most moms, you are always looking for activities that might actually teach
our children something beneficial. Try these ideas.

What Time Is It?

Items Needed:

- Poster board
- Hole puncher
- Felt marker
- Scissors
- Brads

INSTRUCTIONS

Cut a large circle out of the poster board. Write the numbers on the poster board as they would appear on a clock. Cut two arrows from the remaining poster board—one big and one small. Punch holes in the regular end of each one and a hole in the center of the poster board clock. Attach the arrows to the clock with the brad.

Alphabet Art

Items Needed:

- Poster board
- Scissors
- Glue
- Markers or crayons
- Old magazines or grocery store ads

Cut large letters from the poster board and lay a few out on the table at a time. Have your children search through the magazines and ads to find pictures of items that begin with that letter. Then let them cut out the pictures and glue them to the letters they belong to.

Fountains in a Bottle

Items Needed:

- Empty pop bottles
- Vegetable or olive oil
- Food coloring
- Sequins

INSTRUCTIONS

Fill the bottle halfway with water. Add food coloring and sequins. Then fill the bottle the rest of the way with oil. Put on the lid as tightly as possible. As your children shake the bottles, they will be able to see how the contents swirl around and then separate.

Good IDEA

When Dad gets home in the evening, ask your children to explain the concepts they've learned. If Dad isn't available, let them demonstrate these lessons for their friends or grandparents.

another great Idea

Butterfly Book

This is an enchanting activity that can be used for a variety of purposes. Your child may want to use it for practicing his or her name, artwork, names of people to pray for, stickers, or to glue things in. The possibilities are endless.

Items Needed:

- 1 sheet colored construction paper
- 5–10 sheets plain white paper (8x10)
- Crayons, markers, or stickers
- Scissors
- Hole puncher
- Yarn

another great Idea

INSTRUCTIONS

Fold the construction paper in half. Starting and ending on the folded edge, cut out the shape of a wing. It should look like a B. When you unfold the paper, it will be shaped like a butterfly. Using the first piece as a pattern, fold and cut the other sheets of paper (one at a time works best). Punch corresponding holes on the left wings of all the butterflies. Use the yarn to tie the pages together. Let each child decorate his or her own book.

Cool Goopy Stuff

Kids love to stick their fingers in weird textures. Store-bought versions of these "goopy" items are usually appealing, but with the right common household ingredients you can make your own at home on demand. Remind little ones that these elements are intended for the hands and not the mouth.

Finger paint:

2 c. flour
½ c. salt
3 c. boiling water
3 tbsp. oil
Food coloring

Gobbledy Goop:

½ c. liquid starch
1 c. white glue
Food coloring

Silly Dough:

1 c. cornstarch
1 c. white glue

Cost Savers

Many of these ingredients are cheaper if bought in bulk. Find a wholesale outlet that carries items like jars of white glue, large boxes of cornstarch, liquid starch, and construction paper. You'll save some money and have the ingredients on hand when you and the kids feel like you're in the mood for an activity.

LET ME E
N
T
E
R
T
A
I
N

Y
O
U

Let Me Entertain You

Nothing gets a child's imagination racing like an opportunity to perform. It's good for them, too. Young children gain confidence and learn how to overcome shyness. Articulation is improved—there is also the important benefit of learning to laugh at yourself.

Word to the Wise: Teach your children to perform from their hearts as well as their heads by encouraging them to freely express their emotions while performing.

Moms on the Move

Once the stage and puppets are ready, let your children perform to their hearts' content. Help them create simple dialogues between the characters and encourage them to mix and match the puppets as they develop their plays.

Know that this will be more play and less serious performance. That's all right. Your children will entertain themselves and anyone who cares to watch with their puppet antics.

Once the children have become comfortable with the puppets, plan a performance for Dad and/or the grandparents. The primary directive is to "keep it simple." Devise a simple story, such as *The Three Bears*. Schedule ten or fifteen minutes of practice time each afternoon before the performance. Let the children issue the invites over the phone or by creating their own invitations and mailing them.

Ready, set, applaud!

Setting the Stage

Store-bought puppet stages are easy to find and fairly inexpensive.
However, this homemade stage is fun to make and will get the job done.
You and your children can add as many or as few frills as you would like.

Items Needed:

- Refrigerator box
- Contact paper
- Scissors
- Finger paint
- Crayons, markers, or stickers

INSTRUCTIONS

Use the contact paper to cover two sides and the end of a refrigerator box. (You can ask for these at a nearby appliance store.) Lay the box on its side with the papered sides on top and in front. Cut a large hole in the back, the unpapered side big enough for the kids to crawl into. On the opposite side, cut a hole in the top center sector. This should be high enough for the children to crouch below but low enough for them to easily reach with their puppets.

another
great *Idea*

Contact paper comes in many designs, including white. Using white paper will give you and your children an opportunity to do your own decorating. Make sure the box is in the garage or lying on newspapers. Then let your little ones do their best work.

Now it's time to assemble the cast of characters.

Coat Hanger Critters

Items Needed:

- Coat hangers
- Old nylon stockings
- Cloth tape
- Yarn, felt scraps, buttons, wiggly eyes, etc.
- Scissors
- Glue

INSTRUCTIONS

Stretch the hanger into a diamond shape, then pull the stocking over it and tie it at the bottom. Bend the hook into an oval and tape it in place to eliminate the poking hazard. Then help your children decorate their puppets, using the yarn, felt scraps, buttons, and any other odds and ends you think would look good on their creations.

another great Idea

LET ME ENTERTAIN YOU

Animal Masks

Items Needed:

- Styrofoam plates
- Popsicle sticks
- Glue
- Face paint crayons or finger paint
- Crayons
- Colorful yarn or ribbon
- Construction paper
- Scissors
- Paintbrush

another
great Idea

INSTRUCTIONS

Cut an oval shape out of the middle of the plate big enough for your child's eyes, nose, and mouth. Glue a Popsicle stick to the bottom for the child to use as a handle. Use the yarn, ribbon, and construction paper to decorate the plate in the manner of the child's chosen animal. Use the face paint crayons to add eyelashes, whiskers, and other features to your child's face.

Sock Puppets

Popsicle Stick Puppets

Items Needed:

- Old socks
- Craft glue
- Buttons
- Beans
- Yarn
- Scissors

INSTRUCTIONS

Let your children create faces and other features for the puppets using the buttons, beans, and yarn. You can make hair by cutting very small holes in the toe of the sock. Tie a knot at the end of a piece of yarn and feed it through the hole.

Items Needed:

- Popsicle sticks
- Glue
- Construction paper
- Old magazines
- Crayons, markers, or stickers

INSTRUCTIONS

Glue photos, pictures cut from magazines, or hand-drawn pictures to the Popsicle sticks. The children can also decorate their sticks with their own creations using the construction paper and yarn.

Hand Puppets

LET ME ENTERTAIN YOU

Items Needed:

Face paint
Paintbrush

INSTRUCTIONS

Have your children make a fist with their left hands. On the end, use the hole created by the thumb and fingers to represent a mouth. Help your children draw eyes, a nose, and lips to complete the face.

Good IDEA

Allow the children to help you prepare cookies for the events and serve them to their guests once the performance is over.

another great Idea

LET ME ENTERTAIN YOU

Song and Dance Routines

For a wild night of entertainment, encourage your children to dress up (see "Dress-Up Affair" on page 45) and dance and sing to the radio or taped music. Allow each person three or four minutes to be the center of attention with everyone joining in between acts. It's difficult for young children to sit quietly through all the others' routines without a break to get up and get involved.

Urge each child to exercise any specific talents he or she may have, even if these seem to be rather unorthodox to you—multiple somersaults and shining a flashlight in one's mouth is more popular than you might imagine.

another great Idea

Fingerplays

Smaller children may enjoy learning fingerplays such as these:

The Big Brown Bear

The big brown bear walked through the woods.	*(Walk clumsily.)*
She ate some nuts and then some roots.	*(Pretend to eat.)*
It's getting cold today, she thought,	*(Shiver.)*
And off she ran at a fast trot.	*(Run.)*
Then she curled up in her warm den.	*(Curl up.)*
To sleep until it was warm again.	*(Pretend to sleep.)*

Five Little Bears

Five little cubby bears, tumbling on the ground, ... *(Roll hand over in the air.)*

The first one said, "Let's look around." *(Hold up thumb and pretend it's looking around.)*

The second one said, "See the little bunny." *(Hold up index finger and have it point to the bunny. The bunny is made with the index and middle finger of the other hand.)*

The third one said, "I smell honey." . . . . *(Hold up index finger.)*

The fourth one said, "Let's climb a tree." . . . . *(Curl and straighten index finger like a climbing motion.)*

The fifth one said, "Look out! Here come the bees." *(Wiggle little finger, and have fingers of other hand pretend to buzz around it.)*

Five Little Children

(Hold up five fingers; subtract one with each action. Encourage your children to add their own motions to the song.)

Five little children playing on the floor,

 One got tired and then there were four.

Four little children climbing in a tree,

 One jumped down and then there were three.

Three little children skipping to the zoo,

 One went for lunch and then there were two.

Two little children swimming in the pool,

 One went home and then there was one.

One little friend going for a run,

 Decided to take a nap and then there were none.

MOM *Meditations*

Childhood is a magical time, and it passes all too quickly. Treasure every spinning, twirling, running, jumping, let-me-entertain-you moment your child provides. Tuck those memories into your heart. One day when that child calls to say, "Hey, Mom, I passed the bar. . .wrote my first book. . .performed a delicate heart transplant. . . circumnavigated the globe in a hot air balloon"—you will be able to say, "I always knew you would be a star!"

THANK YOU FOR MY FAMILY

Thank You
for My Family

One of the most powerful advantages you can give your children in life is an understanding of the importance of family. Family offers a sense of connectedness, of being part of a whole, of the continuity of life. It affords a security for children and adults alike that cannot be found in any other institution.

Word to the Wise: Your children also need to know that when they live in relationship with God, they are part of the family of God.

That doesn't mean you should despair if you have no family or your family happens to be divided so that interaction is not possible. It is possible to form strong ties with extended family—aunts, uncles, cousins—or even create family ties with surrogate family—friends, godparents, church family.

The point is to raise your children in the knowledge that despite differences and distances, they are far from alone in the world, and they are anchored firmly from one generation to the next.

This chapter will provide you with some activities that will keep family close, even if there are many miles separating you.

Bless Me Bedtime Prayer Chain

Each night when you put your children to bed, let them say their prayers, thanking God for the day, asking for His protection throughout the night and day to follow, and requesting that His blessing be placed on each member of the family. A good way to handle this is by using a family prayer chain.

Items Needed:

- Construction paper
- Scissors
- Markers
- Yarn

INSTRUCTIONS

Fold the construction paper like an accordion. This is the same technique used to create paper dolls. Begin on the left edge, cutting so that one arm goes off the folded edge. Cut in the shape of a stick person—two legs, two arms, a head. When you unfold the paper, your stick people will be attached by one arm. Write the names of family members on each stick person.

If you have a large family, join several chains together by making a small hole in the left arm of the last stick person and a hole in the right arm of another stick person and tying them together with a small piece of yarn.

Let your children color hair and add facial features accordingly. (Yellow hair for Cousin Sue who is a blonde. Red hair for Aunt Sylvia who has flaming locks.) When the people chains are completed, your children can use them during your prayer time to remember each person— God bless Grandma, God bless Grandpa, God bless Aunt Sylvia, God bless Cousin Sue, etc.

Good IDEA

Keep the chain in a special place near your child's bed. Impress on your child that the chain is only for prayer purposes and is not to be played with. Make your child responsible to retrieve the chain at prayer time and return it to its place after prayers.

great another Idea

Small Fry Family Album

All families do not live in close proximity—and even when they do, job moves, illness, injury, or other circumstances may mean your children will be separated from certain family members for significant periods of time. A Small Fry Family Album is a good way to keep mental images sharp and provide comfort and encouragement for your children that the missing person or persons are still in their lives.

Once the photographs have been developed, help your child place them in the album and write the name of the person in marker below the picture. One photo is best for the purposes of this activity.

Items Needed:

- A small photograph album

- Disposable camera

- Marker

Label the album with the child's name: Melissa's Family, Jake's Family, etc. Then, using the disposable camera, help your children take pictures of family members. Try to get shots that are close up enough to easily distinguish the person, and take the picture in the family member's natural surroundings: Papa in his favorite easy chair, Uncle Joe in his truck, Grandma in the kitchen. Take at least two shots of each person in case one of the pictures does not turn out well.

This album should be one that your child can carry around while playing, sleep with at night, and take along on vacation trips. This will not be a coffee table book. Therefore, be sure to choose a small-sized album that appears durable and has plastic inside to cover the photos. Go through the album often and talk to your child about each person, especially those who are far away.

MOM Meditations

It's easy for grieving parents to overlook the pain of a child who has lost a favorite grandparent, aunt, uncle, or close family member. No matter how much you may be hurting, take time to explain to your children that a family member has died, and offer assurances of that person's love. Then use the child's album to talk about the loved one whenever the child feels lonely or sad.

Taped Letter to Grandma

While children are often too distracted or shy to speak to grandparents and other family members on the telephone, they are often gung ho about talking into a microphone or tape recorder, especially if it is presented as a family game.

Items Needed:

- Cassette tape
- Recorder
- Label
- Marker
- Small padded mailing envelope

INSTRUCTIONS

Choose a time when the house is relatively quiet or there are few interruptions—the evening right before bed works well. Hook up the recorder and let your little ones create their own special communication. Begin the tape with an introduction: "Hello. . .this letter is for you from Maggie, Jesse, Annie, and Gayle. It is. . . (day, month, year)."

Make sure your children know whom they are speaking to, and encourage them to speak into the recorder one at a time. Make sure each child begins by saying: "This is (child's name) saying hello," and ends by saying, "This is (child's name) saying good-bye." This sets a benchmark for identification by the listeners. (Voices often sound different on tape.) If the children are slow to speak or don't know what to say, stimulate their monologues by asking questions. You might also suggest that they sing songs, tell jokes, or describe recent events.

Your tape should probably be twenty minutes or less. More than that will seem like a chore to the children and a burden for the listeners. When your tape is complete, label it with names, dates, etc., and mail in a padded mailer.

Kids Can Too!

You might want to enlist the help of an older child to serve as moderator for the taped letter, operating the recorder and helping the younger children record their thoughts.

another
great Idea

75

Book of Love

This is a great activity for teaching children to express their feelings for others. Help them make a "Love Book" whenever they want to say something special to a family member, friend, or even a teacher.

Items Needed:

- Patterned wrapping paper
- Glue
- Scissors
- Pen
- Pencil
- White construction paper
- Stapler or yarn and hole puncher
- Crayons, markers, or stickers

Using the pencil, draw hearts on several different sheets of wrapping paper. Let your children cut them out. Fold the construction paper in half from top to bottom. Cut across the folded paper from bottom to top. You will have two smaller pieces of folded paper. Staple them together on the folded side, or punch three holes along the folded sides, thread the yarn through the holes, and tie off. Glue the hearts to the front of the booklet. Add the name of the person the child wants to give the book to.

On the inside, write one of the following "fill-in-the-blank" questions on each page:

I love _____because _____.

The thing I love most about _____ is _____.

Love makes me feel _____.

Love comes from _____.

I know that _____ loves me, too.

On the back, have your child write his or her name and decorate with hearts, stickers, or original artwork. Down in the bottom corner, put the date or the child's age.

HAPPY

HOLIDAYS

Happy
Holidays

The importance of tradition in our lives and the way we convey it to our children is much more important than some parents imagine. This is nowhere more evident than through the celebration of various holidays.

Word to the Wise: Choose traditions that are meaningful and enjoyable to you and personalize them to make them your own.

On Christmas and Thanksgiving, families gather all over the country. Deep-seated tradition tells them that these are occasions when they should be together. Valentine's Day compels us to say those three little oft neglected words—"I love you." On July 4, we celebrate our freedom, and so on. And on birthdays, we celebrate life itself—specifically the life of a particular person.

Traditions—most often expressed on holidays—keep our feet planted firmly on the ground. They remind us that family, love, freedom, and honoring our parents should not be neglected in the course of our busy lives.

These activities are designed to help you emphasize the meaning of certain holidays for your family. They need not be repeated each year but are intended to help you teach your children the meaning behind a traditional holiday.

Valentine Hearts

Items Needed:

- 12×18-inch piece of red construction paper
- Glue
- Crayons and markers
- Stapler
- White construction paper
- Scissors

INSTRUCTIONS

Fold the red construction paper in half to make a 9×12-inch card. Draw 1×1-inch hearts on the white construction paper. Your children can cut out and glue the hearts to their cards. Once they are positioned on the cards, show the kids how to decorate them by drawing arms, legs, facial features, hair, and other decorations on the hearts.

Write or help your children to write an original verse or one of the following inside the card:

- My heart is full of love for you
  Because of all the things you do.

- Roses are red, violets are blue,
  Sugar is sweet, and so are you!

- Would you, could you,
  please be mine?
  Would you be my valentine?

another
great Idea

Make It Memorable

Many of us have old valentines we've saved from the past. Your children will enjoy seeing the valentines from "your day" and hearing the stories of the people who were important to you as a child.

July 4th
Fly the Flag

Items Needed:

- Finger paint
- Construction paper
- Scissors
- Glue
- Red glitter pens, red crayon, or red marker
- Popsicle sticks
- Decorative sequin stars

great another Idea

INSTRUCTIONS

Find a picture of a flag in a magazine, newspaper, or book. Cut it out and place it where the children can use it for a guide as they work. Cut a rectangle out of construction paper. Color the rectangle by using the blue fingerpaint, red glitter pen, and stars to decorate them. Glue the stick to the back of the flag. When it has had time to dry, write each child's name and age on the back of his or her flag.

Time for Turkeys

Get ready for Thanksgiving by helping your children make their own turkeys.

Items Needed:

- Construction paper
- Finger paint
- Paintbrushes
- Crayons or markers

INSTRUCTIONS

Help your children paint their left palms with brown finger paint. Paint each finger a different color. Then guide them as they press their hands onto the construction paper. When the paint has had time to dry, the kids can use the markers and crayons to add extra detail. Put their names and ages on the back and use these to decorate on Thanksgiving Day.

another
great *Idea*

Santa Claus House

Whether you call this a Santa Claus house or prefer to make it part of a Christmas village, this activity will provide a lot of fun for the children.

Items Needed:

- Graham crackers
- Store-bought white icing
- Red hots, M & Ms, Skittles, or other colorful candies
- Cookie sheet or piece of cardboard
- Food coloring

INSTRUCTIONS

Using the cookie sheet or cardboard as a base, help your children construct the house. The graham crackers are to be used for walls and the roof. Use plenty of icing to hold the house together—it actually makes the house more charming. When your house is standing, stick the candies to the house around doors and windows with icing. You can add food coloring to some of the icing to produce additional colors for your decorating.

Countdown to the Holidays

When it comes to holidays, much of the pleasure is in the anticipation. A countdown calendar is just the thing for helping little ones keep track of what's coming up.

Items Needed:

- Long, white ribbon for each holiday
- Red, green, brown, and white construction paper
- Red and blue colored markers or glitter pens
- Pushpin
- Glue

INSTRUCTIONS

Cut the ribbon in a pretty fashion at the ends. Then use a pushpin to attach it to the wall or a bulletin board. For Valentine's Day, cut hearts out of the red paper and glue them to the ribbon. There should be one for each day leading up to the holiday. Seven to ten days in advance of the holiday is best. For Christmas, cut Christmas trees from the green paper. For Thanksgiving, cut turkeys from the brown paper. For July 4, cut flags from the white paper and let the children decorate them with the pens.

another great Idea

Remove one cutout from the ribbon each day until the holiday arrives—or let your children take turns removing them.

g r e a t another Idea

Kids Can Too!

While you are creating the Countdown Calendar, ask each child to say what he or she thinks the holiday is about. Write down their answers and read them or have one of your children read them to everyone during your holiday celebration.

Moms
on The
Move

Every mom knows the frustration of trying to keep little hands busy while waiting for the doctor, visiting at someone's home, or riding in the car. When on the go, carry along a Big Bag of Activities that will keep kids happily occupied.

Big Bag of Activities

Word to the Wise: Planning on your part can prevent boredom for your kids as well as a lot of stress for you.

You may want to create several folder games—one for matching alphabet letters, one for shapes, and another for matching numbers.

Cut capital and lowercase letters (shapes or numbers) from colored poster board. Glue the capital letters to the inside of the folder. On top of the letters, attach a small piece of self-adhesive Velcro. Attach a small piece of Velcro to the lowercase letters, too. Keep the lowercase letters in a small resealable bag stapled to the inside of the folder. Show the children how to match the lowercase letters to their corresponding capital letters.

Little Hands

"What can we do now?" Garrett asked insistently. Tara looked at her watch. No more than fifteen minutes had passed since she'd helped her four-year-old son and his three-year-old sister start coloring fall leaves on old brown lunch bags. *I'm never going to get these Christmas cards finished,* Tara said to herself with a silent sigh.

Early this morning, when Tara had awakened to gray skies and the sound of a late fall drizzle, she knew the day would be a long one. It was hard to believe that Garrett and Grace had hopped out of bed only three hours ago. Since then, Tara had helped them build a castle out of blocks, fashion zoo animals out of modeling clay, and make handprint turkeys on construction paper to decorate for the upcoming Thanksgiving holiday. Tara was just about out of fresh ideas—and patience.

"Am I five, Mommy?" piped up Grace, interrupting Tara's reverie.

"What, honey?" Tara said, glancing down into Grace's deep brown eyes.

"Am I five now?" Grace repeated adamantly.

"No, sweetie, you're three," Tara said, distracted by a glint of sunshine.

Grace's face registered total disbelief. "Three, still!" she cried out in a shrill tone that captured Tara's full attention.

"Still!" Tara replied. *Guess this day feels as long to her as it does to me!* Tara chuckled privately to herself. Then, with a combination of desperation and motherly enthusiasm, Tara said, "Hey, guys, it looks like the sun might be coming out for a little while. Why don't you put on your rain boots and go splash around in the backyard until lunchtime?"

Before the words had made it out of her mouth, the children had already raced out of the room. *That should give me at least enough time to update that address list.*

As rain gear-clad Grace and Garrett ran off toward the sandbox, Tara closed the backdoor, smiling. She grabbed her favorite blue mug from the kitchen cupboard, made herself a cup of tea, and put on her favorite CD.

In what seemed like no time at all, Tara completed the last address update on the list. *Mission accomplished.* Congratulating herself on a job well done, Tara realized that the CD must have ended awhile ago. The sound of hushed giggles caught her attention. *I didn't even hear the kids come in,* she thought, heading toward the stairs that led up to the children's rooms.

That's when she saw them. Not the kids. The handprints. A border of muddy fingers that led up the white wall to the top of the stairs—to where the children were huddled together, oblivious.

"What do you think you're doing?" Tara exclaimed.

Garrett's giggles stopped abruptly. Grace's turned to tears. As they stood with crayons in their hands, Tara saw that the walls were not only covered with mud but with crayon marks, as well.

"To your rooms!" Tara directed. "Now!"

"But, Mommy," Garrett said timidly, "they're turkeys for Thanksgiving. See the legs?" Deliberately turning away from the wall, Tara bent down to look Garrett directly in the eye. "Go, now."

As the doors of the children's rooms jammed shut, Tara retreated to her own bed. Hot tears spilled down her cheeks, overflowing onto the calico quilt beneath her. *Lord, I can't do this anymore!* Tara couldn't tell whether this was a cry for help or an announcement of her resignation from motherhood. It felt like a bit of both. The one thing Tara was sure of was that without a bit of divine intervention, her kids were going to have a mom who wasn't on the edge, but over it.

As Tara opened her tear-filled eyes, they focused on the plaster cast of four little hands that rested on her nightstand—her Mother's Day gift from her husband after each one of the kids had been born. The hands looked impossibly small, like dolls' hands, instead of hands that real, live children would possess.

Grace's words resounded in Tara's ears.

Am I five yet, Mommy? Three, still!

Not for long. . . Was it God's voice or her own? It didn't matter. What mattered was that it was true. Today was a one-time gift. Tomorrow her children would be older, more independent. Their little hands would be a tiny bit bigger, their feet one step closer to heading out the door on their own. The handprints on the wall could be erased, but the sweet finger-prints on her heart? Never. And she wouldn't want them to be.

Thanks, God, Tara whispered. There was a wall to clean. And it would need a forgiving heart and three sets of hands, both big and small, to tackle the job.

Making Plaster of Paris Handprints

Items Needed:

- Sturdy box lid to use as a mold
- Plaster of paris

Mix plaster of paris according to instructions on the bag. Pour into box lid. Help your child press his or her hand into the plaster and hold it there for 10 seconds. When dry, remove from the mold. Print the following message on a piece of poster board and attach to the dried mold:

another great Idea

"This is (child's name) handprint,

Just so you can recall,

Exactly how my fingers looked

When I was very small."

DATE OR AGE OF CHILD

Also in the

Moms on the Move Series

Family Meals in Minutes

1-59310-209-7

Family Vacations Made Simple

1-59310-211-9

Simple Celebrations

1-59310-210-0

Wherever Books Are Available